Designed by Flowerpot Press
www.FlowerpotPress.com
CHC-0909-0518
ISBN: 978-1-4867-2106-1
Made in China/Fabriqué en Chine

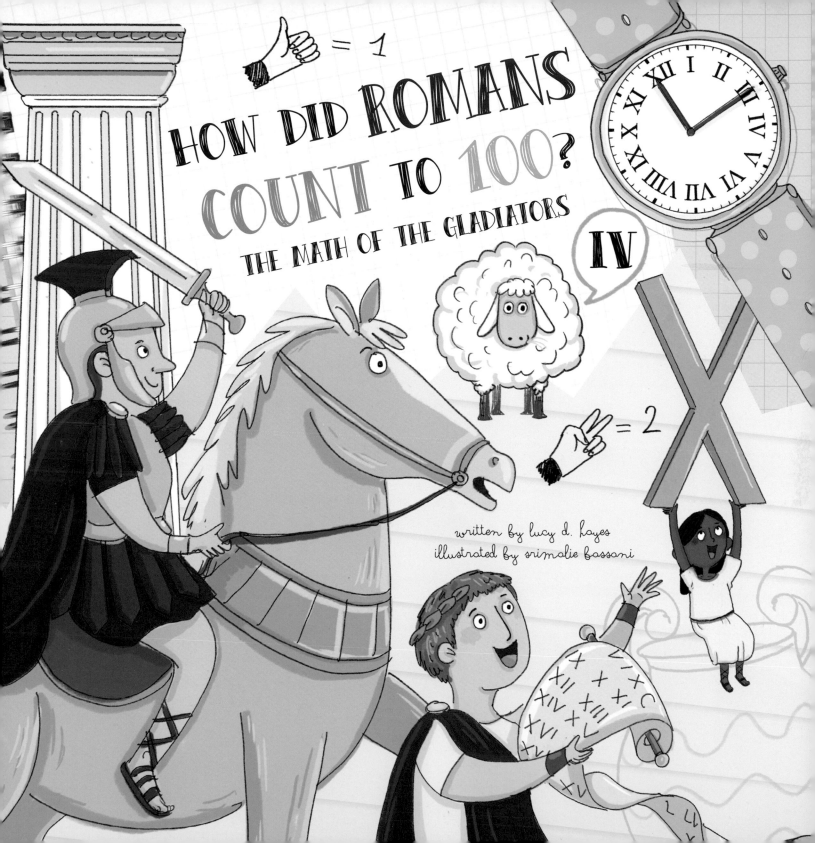

1920

MCMXX

Roman numerals are a way of counting that has existed for thousands of years, and we still use them today. Roman numerals are all around you! They are most commonly used as a fancy way to show how many of something there are. Monarchs have used Roman numerals to signify that they are not the first king or queen to have their name. For example, the current Queen of England is the second Queen of England named Elizabeth, making her Queen Elizabeth II.

The Olympic Games and Super Bowls use Roman numerals to represent how many times the event has been held. For example, the New England Patriots have won Super Bowls XXXVI, XXXVIII, XXXIX, XLIX, LI, and LIII. Hopefully by the end of this book you will know what those symbols mean!

Let's get started and learn how Romans counted to 100!

Capital of Italy
ROME

How did Romans count to 100? It's probably not the way you think...

Romans didn't use the numbers we use today. Ancient Rome was a hub for discovery and around 800 BC, it was decided that discovery would be made easier if there was an agreed upon way to count. You can only use your fingers and toes for so long!

There are multiple theories about how Roman numerals were developed. Some say that they are based on hand signals, while others say they're based on notches etched into sticks for tallying. Either way, the need for a common way to count combined with some creativity and hard work led to the development of Roman numerals.

There are seven symbols used in Roman numerals. They are I, V, X, L, C, D, and M. With these symbols you can make pretty much any number you can think of, except for fractions, decimals, negatives, zero—so maybe there were a few flaws...

Remembering the 7 main Roman numerals can be easier if you use a mnemonic device. Try the one below or try creating your very own.

I Value Xylophones Like Cows Do Milk

I – 1
V – 5
X – 10
L – 50
C – 100
D – 500
M – 1,000

The remaining Roman numerals have developed and changed from other symbols over time, but it has become widely accepted that L represents 50 units, C represents 100 units, D represents 500 units, and M represents 1,000 units.

Now that you know the symbols, there are four key rules that you need to learn in order to put this system of counting to use.

First, if you are trying to write a Roman numeral other than one of the seven you have already learned, you simply combine the symbols together by either adding or subtracting.

RULE NUMBER 1:

When a symbol is repeated, that means you add.

III

I + I + I = III

1 + 1 + 1 = 3

I comes after I so that means you add them together.

Let's learn when you should add. Rule number one says when the same symbol repeats, that means you need to add them together. For example, when you see the Roman numeral III, you know to add because the Roman numeral I is repeated. I+I+I=III or 1+1+1=3.

If there is a sequence of Roman numerals and a smaller symbol comes after a larger symbol, that means you need to follow rule number two and add. For example, the Roman numeral VI means that you are adding the smaller Roman numeral (I) to the larger Roman numeral (V). V+I=VI or 5+1=6.

Sometimes Roman numerals require you to use both rules. For example, the Roman numeral for 7 looks like this: VII. First you see that the smaller symbol (I) is after the larger symbol (V), so you know you need to add them together. Then there are repeating symbols (II) which also means you need to add. V+I+I=VII or 5+1+1=7.

Since you now know that the Roman numeral for 3 is III, you may think that the Roman numeral for 4 is IIII, but this is where the third rule comes in.

The third rule says that you can never have more than three of the same symbol in a row. So how do you make the number 4? You follow rule number four! First you take the symbol for 1 (I) and place it to the left of the symbol for 5 (V) in a series like this: IV. Placing smaller symbols to the left of larger symbols works as a form of subtraction. 5-1=4 or V-I= IV.

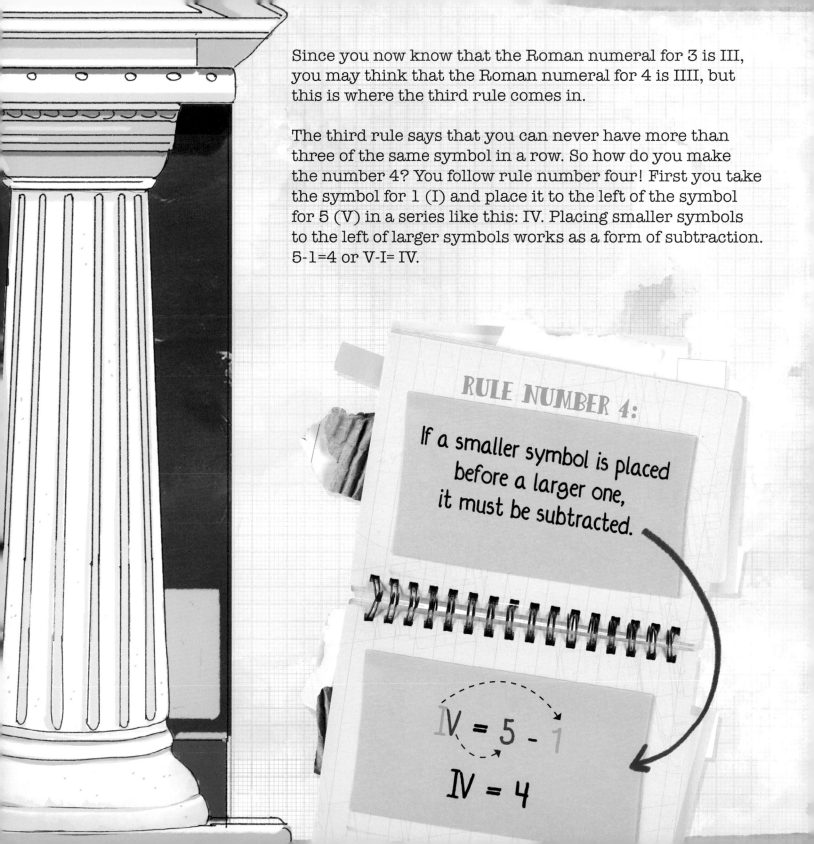

RULE NUMBER 4:

If a smaller symbol is placed before a larger one, it must be subtracted.

IV = 5 - 1

IV = 4

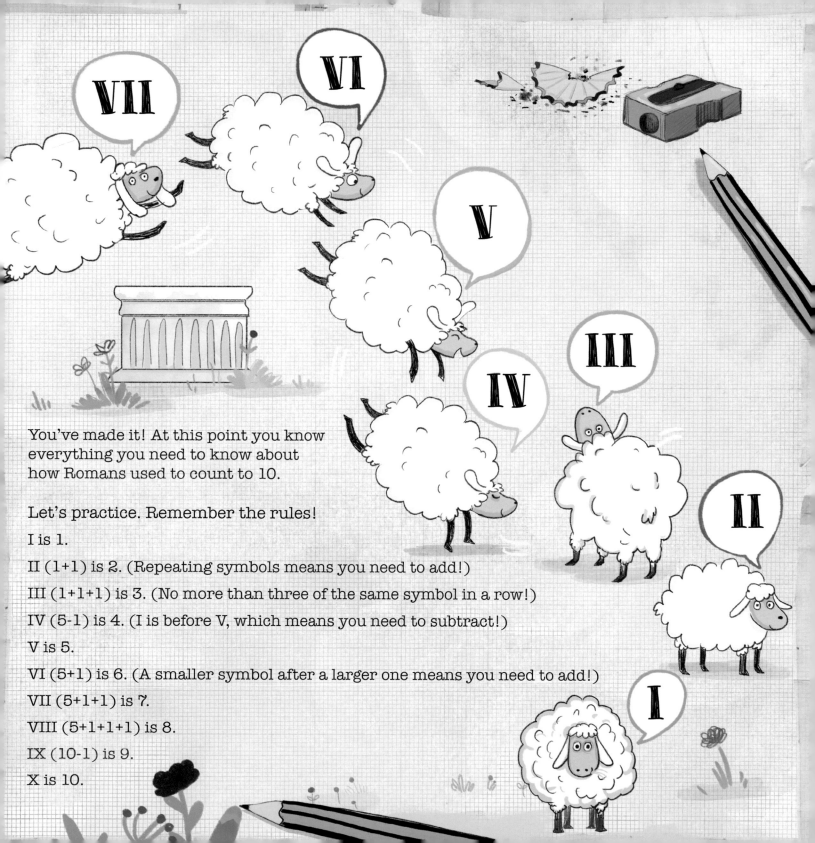

You've made it! At this point you know everything you need to know about how Romans used to count to 10.

Let's practice. Remember the rules!

I is 1.

II (1+1) is 2. (Repeating symbols means you need to add!)

III (1+1+1) is 3. (No more than three of the same symbol in a row!)

IV (5-1) is 4. (I is before V, which means you need to subtract!)

V is 5.

VI (5+1) is 6. (A smaller symbol after a larger one means you need to add!)

VII (5+1+1) is 7.

VIII (5+1+1+1) is 8.

IX (10-1) is 9.

X is 10.

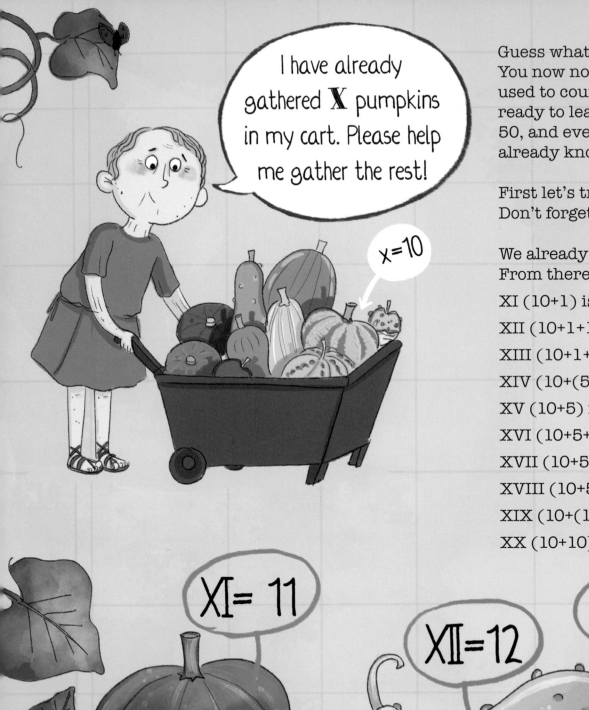

Guess what? You can keep going! You now not only know how Romans used to count to 10, but now you're ready to learn how to count to 20, 50, and even 100 using what you already know!

First let's try counting to 20. Don't forget the rules!

We already know X represents 10. From there...

XI (10+1) is 11.

XII (10+1+1) is 12.

XIII (10+1+1+1) is 13.

XIV (10+(5-1)) is 14.

XV (10+5) is 15.

XVI (10+5+1) is 16.

XVII (10+5+1+1) is 17.

XVIII (10+5+1+1+1) is 18.

XIX (10+(10-1)) is 19.

XX (10+10) is 20.

Now let's try counting to 100 by tens using the symbols and rules you've learned.

Give it a try!

X is 10.

XX (10+10) is 20.

XXX (10+10+10) is 30.

XL (50-10) is 40.

L is 50.

LX (50+10) is 60.

LXX (50+10+10) is 70.

LXXX (50+10+10+10) is 80.

XC (100-10) is 90.

And C is 100.

=10

50-10=40

=50

50+10+10+10=80

ROMAN NUMERALS

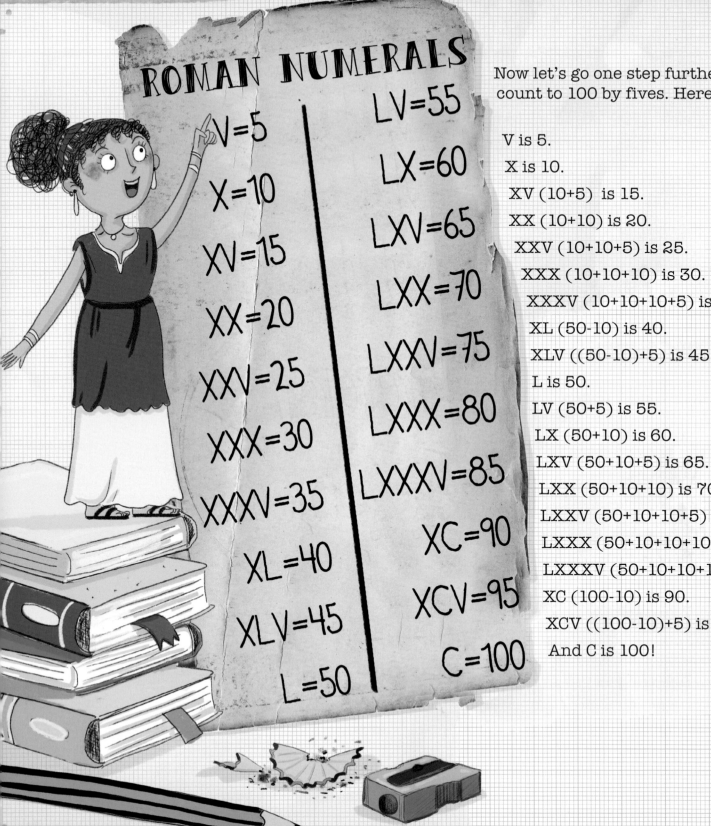

V = 5

X = 10

XV = 15

XX = 20

XXV = 25

XXX = 30

XXXV = 35

XL = 40

XLV = 45

L = 50

LV = 55

LX = 60

LXV = 65

LXX = 70

LXXV = 75

LXXX = 80

LXXXV = 85

XC = 90

XCV = 95

C = 100

Now let's go one step further and count to 100 by fives. Here we go!

V is 5.

X is 10.

XV (10+5) is 15.

XX (10+10) is 20.

XXV (10+10+5) is 25.

XXX (10+10+10) is 30.

XXXV (10+10+10+5) is 35.

XL (50-10) is 40.

XLV ((50-10)+5) is 45.

L is 50.

LV (50+5) is 55.

LX (50+10) is 60.

LXV (50+10+5) is 65.

LXX (50+10+10) is 70.

LXXV (50+10+10+5) is 75.

LXXX (50+10+10+10) is 80.

LXXXV (50+10+10+10+5) is 85.

XC (100-10) is 90.

XCV ((100-10)+5) is 95.

And C is 100!

38 63 29
37 87 74
46 52 99

Are you able to write these numbers in Roman numerals?

LET'S PRACTICE! What do you think the Roman numeral for 38 is? What about 63? Before turning the page, grab a piece of paper and a pencil and write down how to write the numbers above as Roman numerals. Turn the page to check your work.

38 is XXXVIII

$$10+10+10+5+1+1+1=38$$

37 is XXXVII

$$10+10+10+5+1+1=37$$

74 is LXXIV

$$50+10+10+(5-1)=74$$

46 is XLVI

$$(50-10)+5+1=46$$

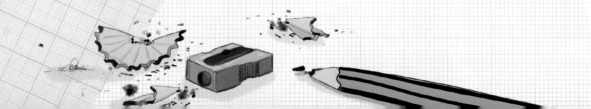

63 is (LXIII)

$50+10+1+1+1=63$

29 is (XXIX)

$10+10+(10-1)=29$

87 is (LXXXVII)

$50+10+10+10+5+1+1=87$

Now you can use the same system
to count to 100 just like a Roman!

52 is (LII)

$50+1+1=52$

99 is (XCIX)

$100-10+(10-1)=99$

ROMAN NUMERALS ARE ALL AROUND US

You can find Roman numerals all around you if you take the time to look. Here are some examples of how Roman numerals are still used today.

Modern day architecture will occasionally mark the date a building or statue was erected using Roman numerals. Many times you can find Roman numerals on government buildings, like courthouses.

Roman numerals can be seen on the Statue of Liberty! The numbers represent the adoption date of the United States Declaration of Independence. And did you know that Lady Liberty was even modeled after a Roman goddess named Libertas?

Clocks and watches sometimes have Roman numerals on their faces. You may notice that many clocks that use Roman numerals will write 4 as IIII. Nobody is entirely sure why, but it seems to be based on how Roman numerals were initially written without a system involving subtraction.

CHAPTER I

Books and plays that use Roman numerals for acts, chapters, and volumes often use this technique because it has been used this way for many, many years. Since using Roman numerals was a standard in books and plays, it remains a popular choice today.

I'm Queen Elizabeth II, **SECOND** of my name.

William Barnaby Elliot III

When somebody has the same name as somebody else in their family, they need an easy way to differentiate themselves. Since many naming computer systems do not allow symbols, it makes sense to use Roman numerals as they can be written using English letters.

ROMAN NUMERALS WITH TOOTHPICKS

Practice making Roman numerals using toothpicks. You should ask an adult for help before trying this activity.

What you'll need:

30 toothpicks
White paper

How it works:

1. Lay out your piece of paper horizontally on a table.

2. Ask an adult or friend to write 3 numbers from 1-10 on the paper. Be sure to space out the numbers and leave room below each one for you to try making your Roman numerals.

3. Below each number, lay out your toothpicks to create the Roman numeral equivalent. (For example, if the paper says 7, you will need four toothpicks. Two will be in the shape of a V and two will go directly after the V vertically.)

4. Continue using the toothpicks to create the Roman numerals for the remaining numbers on the paper.

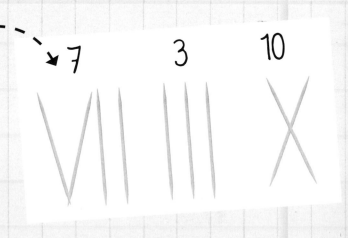

Once you have mastered numbers 1–10, try creating Roman numerals for numbers up to 50! Refer to the chart on the final page if you need any hints.

ROMAN NUMERAL DECODING

Using a piece of paper and a pencil, try decoding the phrases below using the key.

What you'll need:
Pencil
Paper

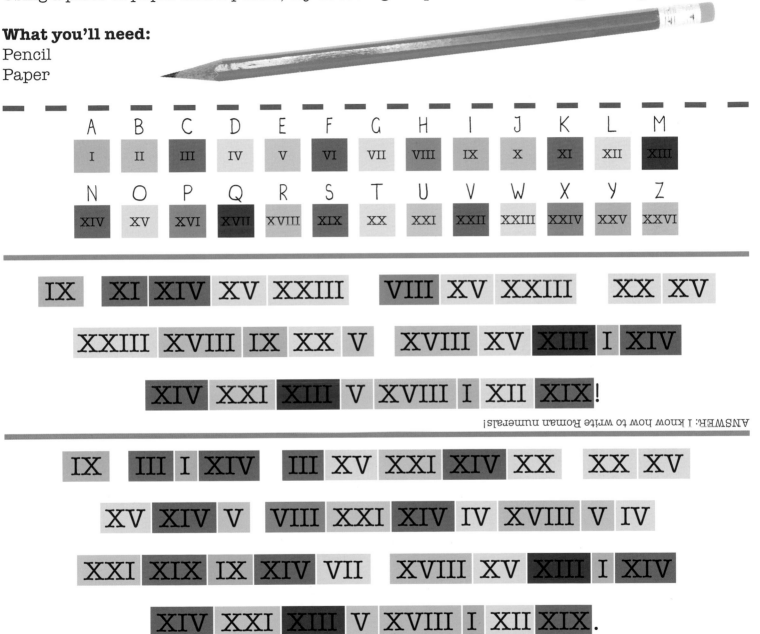

A	B	C	D	E	F	G	H	I	J	K	L	M
I	II	III	IV	V	VI	VII	VIII	IX	X	XI	XII	XIII

N	O	P	Q	R	S	T	U	V	W	X	Y	Z
XIV	XV	XVI	XVII	XVIII	XIX	XX	XXI	XXII	XXIII	XXIV	XXV	XXVI

IX   XI XIV XV XXIII   VIII XV XXIII   XX XV

XXIII XVIII IX XX V   XVIII XV XIII I XIV

XIV XXI XIII V XVIII I XII XIX!

IX   III I XIV   III XV XXI XIV XX   XX XV

XV XIV V   VIII XXI XIV IV XVIII V IV

XXI XIX IX XIV VII   XVIII XV XIII I XIV

XIV XXI XIII V XVIII I XII XIX.

Try creating your own codes for your friends to solve using the key above. Then try writing codes using letters and writing the corresponding Roman numerals instead!

ROMAN NUMERAL CHART

1	**I**	21	**XXI**	41	**XLI**	61	**LXI**	81	**LXXXI**
2	**II**	22	**XXII**	42	**XLII**	62	**LXII**	82	**LXXXII**
3	**III**	23	**XXIII**	43	**XLIII**	63	**LXIII**	83	**LXXXIII**
4	**IV**	24	**XXIV**	44	**XLIV**	64	**LXIV**	84	**LXXXIV**
5	**V**	25	**XXV**	45	**XLV**	65	**LXV**	85	**LXXXV**
6	**VI**	26	**XXVI**	46	**XLVI**	66	**LXVI**	86	**LXXXVI**
7	**VII**	27	**XXVII**	47	**XLVII**	67	**LXVII**	87	**LXXXVII**
8	**VIII**	28	**XXVIII**	48	**XLVIII**	68	**LXVIII**	88	**LXXXVIII**
9	**IX**	29	**XXIX**	49	**XLIX**	69	**LXIX**	89	**LXXXIX**
10	**X**	30	**XXX**	50	**L**	70	**LXX**	90	**XC**
11	**XI**	31	**XXXI**	51	**LI**	71	**LXXI**	91	**XCI**
12	**XII**	32	**XXXII**	52	**LII**	72	**LXXII**	92	**XCII**
13	**XIII**	33	**XXXIII**	53	**LIII**	73	**LXXIII**	93	**XCIII**
14	**XIV**	34	**XXXIV**	54	**LIV**	74	**LXXIV**	94	**XCIV**
15	**XV**	35	**XXXV**	55	**LV**	75	**LXXV**	95	**XCV**
16	**XVI**	36	**XXXVI**	56	**LVI**	76	**LXXVI**	96	**XCVI**
17	**XVII**	37	**XXXVII**	57	**LVII**	77	**LXXVII**	97	**XCVII**
18	**XVIII**	38	**XXXVIII**	58	**LVIII**	78	**LXXVIII**	98	**XCVIII**
19	**XIX**	39	**XXXIX**	59	**LIX**	79	**LXXIX**	99	**XCIX**
20	**XX**	40	**XL**	60	**LX**	80	**LXXX**	100	**C**
200	**CC**	300	**CCC**	400	**CD**	500	**D**	600	**DC**
700	**DCC**	800	**DCCC**	900	**CM**	1,000	**M**	5,000	**$\overline{\text{V}}$**
10,000	**$\overline{\text{X}}$**	50,000	**$\overline{\text{L}}$**	100,000	**$\overline{\text{C}}$**	500,000	**$\overline{\text{D}}$**	1,000,000	**$\overline{\text{M}}$**

Remember when we said you would know which Super Bowl titles the New England Patriots have won? Use the chart and what you've learned to see if you can figure it out!